# Basics of Supporting Dual Language Learners

## An Introduction for Educators of Children from Birth through Age 8

Karen N. Nemeth

National Association for the Education of Young Children

Washington, DC

National Association for the Education
of Young Children
1313 L Street NW, Suite 500
Washington, DC 20005-4101
202-232-8777 • 800-424-2460
www.naeyc.org

**NAEYC Books**

Chief Publishing Officer
*Derry Koralek*

Editor-in-Chief
*Kathy Charner*

Director of Creative Services
*Edwin C. Malstrom*

Senior Editor
*Holly Bohart*

Design and Production
*Malini Dominey*

Assistant Editor
*Elizabeth Wegner*

Editorial Assistant
*Ryan Smith*

Through its publications program, the National Association for the Education of Young Children (NAEYC) provides a forum for discussion of major issues and ideas in the early childhood field, with the hope of provoking thought and promoting professional growth. The views expressed or implied in this book are not necessarily those of the Association or its members.

Cover and inside illustrations by David Clark.
Contributing editors: *Steve Olle and Catherine Cauman*

**Basics of Supporting Dual Language Learners: An Introduction for Educators of Children from Birth through Age 8**

Copyright © 2012 by the National Association for the Education of Young Children. All rights reserved. Printed in the United States of America.

Library of Congress Control Number: 2012934863
ISBN: 978-1-928896-84-5
NAEYC Item #366

# About the Author

**Karen N. Nemeth**, Ed.M., is an author, consultant, and presenter who focuses on first and second language development in young children. She works with individual early childhood programs and districts on improving their supports for dual language learners. She has written for *Young Children*, *Teaching Young Children*, and *Child Care Information Exchange* and is an NAEYC Consulting Editor. She is also on the board of NJTESOL-NJBE (New Jersey Teachers of English to Speakers of Other Languages/New Jersey Bilingual Educators).

Nemeth is the author of *Many Languages, One Classroom: Teaching Dual and English Language Learners* and *Many Languages, Building Connections: Supporting Infants and Toddlers Who Are Dual Language Learners*. She hosts a resource sharing website at www. languagecastle.com.

# Contents

# About This Book

According to the 2010 United States Census, close to a quarter of the young children in this country are growing up in families where English is not the primary language. Chances are, at some point in your early childhood career, you will work with children and families who speak a language that is not familiar to you. This book is designed to help all early childhood educators learn the basics of developmentally appropriate teaching practices for young children who are dual language learners (DLLs).

## Purpose and audience

This book, part of the NAEYC Basics series, pulls together in one manageable volume the most important information needed by any program serving children and families who use diverse languages. Administrators, teachers, assistants, social workers, and family workers can read and refer to this book as they create and carry out a shared vision for how their program will support the learning and development of children who speak different languages.

Directors and principals will learn what they need to provide for classrooms and what developmentally appropriate strategies they should support. Teachers will learn how to adapt their practices and implement a curriculum to help DLLs reach their learning potential. Bilingual teachers and teaching assistants will find ideas for using their multiple language assets effectively to support children's learning and engage families. Social workers and family workers will learn about the research and policies on supporting DLLs and their families so they can encourage appropriate language and literacy supports in the home.

## What's in this book?

Part I "Understanding Dual Language Learners" offers information on first and second language development and the value of supporting the home language. Part II "Strategies for Supporting Dual Language Learners" includes a classroom checklist, techniques that work when the practitioner doesn't speak the same languages as the children, techniques for bilingual practitioners who do, and guidance for directors and administrators on supporting their staff. The answers to frequently asked questions will connect the reader to real-life situations in which early childhood practitioners apply solutions to unique circumstances.

This volume provides a brief introduction to the topic. As you get to know more about the research-based information and strategies offered here, you may want to build your knowledge specific to the children and families with whom you work. You will find a variety of relevant professional development resources at the end of the book to fit your needs and interests.

Whether you are an experienced early childhood educator or new to the field, this volume provides relevant information that will enable you to meet the needs of young children who are dual language learners with success.

# Understanding Dual Language Learners

# What Is a Dual Language Learner?

*Dual language learner* is a term used to describe children who are growing up with two (or more) languages. This can happen in many ways. For example, Jada is growing up with a mom who speaks English and a dad who speaks Mandarin. In Jackson's family, both parents speak English, but his grandma who visits several times a week speaks to Jackson in Polish. José grew up speaking Spanish at home and never heard English until he started school. Joon comes from a home where Korean is used primarily, but family members and neighbors also expose him to English.

It is important to note, that regardless of their different circumstances, all children under the age of 6 are at some stage of developing language. Whether they are saying more in their first language or understanding more in their second, or excelling or struggling in both languages, all young children need support of their entire language development spectrum.

Many early childhood programs and school districts use the term *English language learner* (ELL) to describe a child who is learning English as a second language. Some educators believe this term focuses on the learning of English as if the home language is something to be left behind. We know that young children need continuing support of their home language while they are also learning English (Castro et al. 2011). And, in the first four years, even children who are exposed only to English could be considered English language learners because they are all working on learning how to speak and understand English.

The term *bilingual* generally refers to the skills of a person who has developed fluency in two languages. Some experts use the term only to refer to people who have developed full use of the second language equivalent to their native language, but other experts use it to describe anyone who is in the process of learning to use a second language (Gottardo & Grant 2008). We also use bilingual to describe experiences or environments that provide information in two languages. Some individuals develop the ability to speak and understand a second language, but they may not be *biliterate* (able to read and write in both languages). Because young children are not yet fluent in any language, they would not be considered fully bilingual. You could say that dual language learners are developing both of their languages through their bilingual environment.

By using "dual language learners," we make it clear that developmentally appropriate early care and education focuses on all of a child's early language experience—and cultural experience as well. When children participate in group or individual experiences with adults and other children who speak English, their proficiency in that language will grow over time. This happens in part because they are exposed to English in their environment and because each child has unique abilities and an individual pace of development. Nevertheless, their home language is still the language of their family, their culture, and many of the things they learned in that context, so home languages must continue to be recognized and supported well into the school years (Espinosa 2010).

> Dual language learners (DLLs) are young children who are growing up with two or more languages.

For the first four years of his life, Josué lived on a farm in Brazil. When his family moved to the United States and enrolled him in preschool, he found himself in an English-speaking environment for the first time. Although Josué had never been to school before, he knew much about the different plants on his farm—what they needed to grow and stay healthy, how to count them and sort them, what different colors may mean in different fruits or vegetables. And he learned many songs with his parents as they brought him along to tend the farm. However, Josué experienced all of this knowledge in Portuguese.

He knew many things, but he did not know them in English. There was no connection to farming in his new school, so he could not share all of his wonderful knowledge with his new teachers and friends.

One day, the teacher invited a student from the local high school to read to Josué in Portuguese. Soon the two were having detailed conversations about things Josué remembered from his former home and family life. Feeling more confident than he had in a while, Josué began to sing one of his mother's favorite songs, and the visitor joined in. When the visitor related some of the conversation to the teacher, she was amazed. She began to realize that getting to know Josué would mean finding ways to understand the language and culture he brought with him—not just teaching him new concepts and words in English.

Today the term dual language learners is used by NAEYC, the Office of Head Start, and the Council for Exceptional Children Division for Early Childhood. These key national organizations have taken a leadership role in recognizing the value of diversity in the lives of young children and encouraging programs to celebrate the unique language and cultural background of each child as an individual.

# Understanding the Value of Supporting the Home Language

When implementing strategies for teaching DLLs in early care and education, it is important to understand why these strategies include strong support of the home language along with scaffolding the development of English skills. There are four main reasons that encompass all developmental domains.

## The home language supports cognitive development

Most of what young children know when they start at a program or school has already been learned and remembered in the home language. Thus, much of what you teach in early childhood is based on each child's prior knowledge. Supporting young children's continued use and development of their home language enables them to have full use of what they know in that language while they are also building concepts and connections in English. At any given time, a DLL child will know and understand some things in connection with one language and some things in the other.

For example, a child who learns what red is will recognize the color no matter what language the teacher is using to talk to him about a red shirt. At the same time, it is also true that he will be thinking the word *red* when he sees the color, or he might think *rojo* if he learned the Spanish word to associate with the color. When early education environments include opportunities for DLLs to use their prior knowledge in their home language, it may be easier for them to use that foundation of knowledge to learn new things.

José knows the word *ear* and the word *eye* and can accurately point to those body parts when asked by his English-speaking teacher. She is a little surprised that he is 3 and knows only two body parts. Meanwhile, when the Spanish-speaking assistant teacher talks with him, she notices he correctly responds to *la boca* (mouth) and *la nariz* (nose). Only after the teacher and assistant discuss his progress do they realize José is not developing slowly—he actually knows four body parts. It was the limited language they used to ask questions that made it seem to each of them that he knew only two.

Research (Espinosa 2010) has shown that children can easily transfer early literacy skills developed in the home language to a new language.

Hemal's parents are from India and they speak Gujerati at home. They have taught Hemal children's chants and songs in their home language that have helped her learn to pay attention to the rhythm and syllables of speech in Gujerati. This practice has made it easier for her to listen for the rhythm and syllables in her new language, too. She already understands that the sounds and how you say them create meaningful words. Learning new words in a new language is just a different way of doing the same kind of learning for Hemal.

Many experts recommend that DLLs should begin to learn to read in their home language if that is the one they use most. Once a child has learned to read, he can use his reading skills to learn in a new language. It is not always easy for children to learn the alphabet. However, once a child catches on to the idea that words are made up of written symbols, each symbol has a name and a sound, and these symbols are combined in different ways to make words, she can readily learn a second or third alphabet system.

Growing up bilingual provides additional, lasting benfits: "The advantages of being bi- or multilingual go beyond the family. Research has shown that children who are fluent in two languages enjoy certain cognitive advantages in comparison to those who speak only one language. For example, they are better at problem solving, demonstrate greater creativity, and express more tolerant attitudes toward others (Bialystok & Martin 2004; Genesee & Gandara 1999)" (Genesee 2008, 17).

## The home language encourages self-esteem

Educators are typically concerned about the ways in which learning in more than one language may affect the cognitive, academic, and literacy progress of DLLs. They may focus on the relationship between language and learning, but language development is important in other areas of the child's development as well. For each of us, our language is part of who we are—part of our basic identity. From the very beginning, children come to understand who they are as individuals and as family members. Children's language is as much a part of them as their name, their home, their family traditions, and their connections to their parents and siblings. When children grow up with a non-English language as part of their identity and then come to a program or school where that language is not used, they may feel that a part of them is neither valued nor liked.

> Miss Susan made it a point to remember each child's birthday and the name of their siblings and their pets. She viewed this as a way to support children's self-esteem by showing how important they are to her. Jeanette's mom visited the classroom one day and noticed the teacher seemed to know more about the other children than she did about Jeanette, who spoke mostly Haitian Creole. Jeanette's mom mentioned this to the teacher. "What an eye-opener," said Miss Susan. "I realized I really was making Jeanette feel like a second-class citizen in my classroom because I didn't understand her language. I asked her mom to help me learn more about their language and family activities so I could be a better support for Jeanette."

**The home language**
- supports cognitive development
- encourages self-esteem
- strengthens family ties
- enhances social interactions

> "When parents are unable to talk to their children, they cannot easily convey to them their values, beliefs, understandings, or wisdom about how to cope with their experiences. They cannot teach them about the meaning of work, or about personal responsibility, or what it means to be a moral or ethical person in a world with too many choices and too few guideposts to follow. What is lost are the bits of advice, the *consejos* parents should be able to offer children in their everyday interactions with them. Talk is a crucial link between parents and children: It is how parents impart their cultures to their children and enable them to become the kind of men and women they want them to be. When parents lose the means for socializing and influencing their children, rifts develop and families lose the intimacy that comes from shared beliefs and understandings." (Wong Fillmore 1991, 343)

From: Wong Fillmore, L. 1991. When learning a second language means losing the first. *Early Childhood Research Quarterly* 6 (3): 323–46.

Just as it is important to learn each child's name, his likes and dislikes, his fears and interests, and the people in his family, it is equally important that teachers and assistants get to know and show their respect for his language. Every young child should see some oral and written representation of their home language and culture in the place where they spend so many hours away from home. You will find a number of suggestions for doing this effectively as you read this book.

## The home language strengthens family ties

When children see that their home language is important and valued by others, they are less likely to leave it behind as they strive to fit in by learning English. Losing the ability to really communicate with each other can be heartbreaking for families. Even if children and parents begin to speak more English, it can be a significant loss when they are no longer able to talk with their grandparents or other loved ones who speak the home language.

> On the first day of second grade, Luis corrected his teacher, "My name is Loo-iss, not Loo-ees." He appeared to be fluent in English so the teacher realized she must have been wrong when she assumed he was a native Spanish speaker. Later that same day, Luis became ill and vomited in the classroom. Not only was he in pain, but he was embarrassed as well because the other children made quite a fuss. The school nurse called his home to have him picked up. When his grandmother arrived, it became clear that she spoke little English. They walked out in silence and Luis was unable to share his misery— to explain that his pride hurt far more than his stomachache.

Why is helping children maintain their home language an important concern for early care and education programs? Consider how educators emphasize the importance of family involvement in schools to help children achieve academic success. Supporting strong families is important for all who work in the early childhood field. Maintaining the home language is a way to keep the lines of communication open between parents and children, thus helping children grow up with a healthy sense of family bonding and support.

## The home language enhances social interactions

In some programs the adults speak only English but only some of the children speak English, too. The children who do not speak the language of the teachers may feel less important or less valued. That is certainly not an ideal environment for learning and developing.

When children who speak different languages are in school together, they typically live in nearby neighborhoods together, and they need to grow up learning to respect each other and to get along. When every classroom—from infant/toddler programs through elementary school—provides an environment that celebrates diversity, all of the children can grow up seeing each other as equals.

When Paola joined the 2-year-olds group at the child care center, she was beginning to speak her native Italian, but no English. Her teachers did not know Italian, and Paola did not respond to most of their attempts to talk to her in English. The English-speaking children generally responded so well that the teachers really enjoyed playing with, cuddling with, and reading to them.

One day the director came to observe and noticed that little Paola was often left out—not only by the teachers but by the other children as well. They were beginning to talk to each other, as 2-year-olds do, but they seemed to push right past Paola as if she was a piece of furniture. And she seemed unhappy. The director asked the teachers if she could videotape a portion of their day and show it to them later. When she showed the video to the teachers they were able to see that their behavior had influenced the children's behavior. They talked to the director about resources that would help them learn better ways to support Paola and to be better role models for the other children.

## Getting to know families who speak different languages

Clearly, there are many reasons why supporting each child's home language is important. To achieve this goal, every teacher, assistant, administrator, and social worker needs to know which languages are spoken in each child's home. Once a child has been enrolled, staff can use a language survey to learn about the family's home language. Paper and pencil surveys don't always yield the full picture. Additional interactions such as home visits or phone conversations may help staff gain a better understanding of the child's language environment so the program can prepare the classroom and the teaching staff accordingly.

It is not enough to say a child "comes from China." You need to know if his family speaks Mandarin, Cantonese, or one of the many other Chinese languages and dialects. Assumptions based on a person's last name or appearance are often incorrect. The more accurate information you have, the more appropriately you can meet each child's needs.

# First Language Development

**U**nderstanding how the brain learns and processes the first language is a key piece to the puzzle of second language development. All children progress through the stages described here, regardless of the language being learned. However, there may be great differences between children in terms of how fast they move from stage to stage, or how many words they add to their vocabulary as they progress.

It is important to remember that there is no strong evidence to show that growing up in a bilingual environment slows a child's language development. Any child may experience slowing or speeding up at different stages, but given enough language stimulation in the early years, DLLs generally have basic language skills equal to their monolingual peers as they progress through elementary school (Han 2012).

Keep in mind that DLL children who have a true language delay or disorder will show signs in both of their languages because these issues are caused by biological or developmental factors that compromise the entire language learning system. If a child shows delay in only one language, it is likely due to environmental factors. These factors might include a child who gets more input in one language than the other, a child who feels shy and doesn't want to speak in school even though he has the ability to speak, or a child growing up with a parent who is depressed and doesn't encourage much talking at home (Paradis et al. 2011).

> Mr. Smith was concerned that 3-year-old Asad did not say much in his preschool class. He was thinking about discussing the situation with Asad's family and possibly suggesting a referral for evaluation. But one day he watched Asad leave school with his mom and sister. All three were chattering away in animated conversation in their home language. He realized that Asad was developing lots of language skills, but he wasn't comfortable speaking in his home language or in English while at school.

## Stages of first language development

**Crying (0–3 months).** Although newborn infants are able to communicate only through crying, they reveal much about their extraordinary ability to learn and process language. They make different kinds of cries to express their different needs—complete with variety in tone, pitch, pace, and even body language. Researchers have found that infant brains are already cataloging the sounds they hear in the language around them (Kuhl 2010). When their parents and caregivers talk to them, infants begin to focus on useful sounds and ignore sounds that don't occur regularly.

**Cooing (3–6 months).** As infants learn that they can control their voice even when they are not crying, they love to produce cooing sounds that are mostly vowels like "ooooh" and "aaah." They may not talk, but they already know how to take turns, being quiet when an adult talks to them and then making sounds when the adult becomes quiet.

**Babbling (6–12 months).** Around the seventh month, infants begin to add consonants to their vocalizations. Even at this early stage, there are differences between the babbling of infants who grow up with different languages. Well before they say their first word, infants have already developed a sophisticated understanding of what sounds they need to practice and what sounds they can stop using. They also become experts at using tone of voice, gestures, facial expressions, and body language to help adults understand their meaning.

**First words (10–14 months).** By the time toddlers are ready to say their first word, they have already learned so much about language that they choose first words for very specific purposes. They learn to call out for mama or dada or papa—the people who can meet their needs. No matter how many times a day, or with how much excitement you say their own name to them, infants never learn to say their own name first. They don't start with the words they hear most often in their environment such as *and* or *the*. They begin with words that interest them or get them what they need or want. That reveals an amazing grasp of the language well before children ever say their first word. And that first word comes from what's developing in the child's mind—not from lessons or flash cards or rewards or punishments. This is how the brain supports language learning. Children's brains catalog the sounds of speech around them and then practice the parts that communicate their wants and needs. Early childhood practitioners need to keep that fact in mind as they plan their strategies for supporting the language development of all young children, but especially DLLs.

**One word at a time (10–18 months).** Once children say their first words, they generally speak one word at a time for about six months until they begin putting words together. During this phase, children's one-word utterances usually carry the same meaning as a whole phrase or sentence. For example, if a toddler comes into the kitchen and says "Wawa? Wawa?" you might say, "Oh! Do you want some water?" You assume that the child is not simply practicing his *w* sound—he has something in mind and he says it with a questioning tone of voice—so you interpret that one word as a request for a drink of water. Again we see that the child's brain is working hardest at establishing communication and getting needs met.

**Two words together (17–20 months).** After saying their first words, it generally takes about six months for children to be developmentally ready to put two words together. We call this phase *telegraphic speech* because toddlers do not just

Stages of First Language Development
- 0–3 Months: Crying
- 3–6 Months: Cooing
- 6–12 Months: Babbling
- 10–14 Months: First Words
- 10–18 Months: One Word at a Time
- 17–20 Months: Two Words Together
- 2–5 Years: Language Explosion

use the two first words of a sentence or the two easiest words to say—they create two-word sentences that capture the most important meaning they want to convey. Instead of saying "the truck," they might say "truck go" or "MY truck." In the olden days you had to pay for each word to send a telegram, so people were careful to get the most meaning with the fewest words—just like toddlers' language at this stage! Older children repeat this stage as they learn a second language.

**Language explosion (2–5 years).** Once young children begin to put two words together in short sentences and phrases, their language development typically takes off. They have already learned about the rules of language and taking turns and how to use tone of voice and gesture to add meaning. Now they spend most of their mental energy learning new concepts about how the world works. They learn the words that help them make sense of those concepts and use their new vocabulary to communicate the concepts to others. Throughout the first five years, children will always understand more than they can say.

> In the infant/toddler room, Maria says "Bah!" Ms. Jeannine says "That's a good idea! Let's read a book! Give me the book and we'll read it together." Maria repeats "bah" then toddles over to Ms. Jeannine's chair and hands her the book.

Adults should speak to children's level of understanding (their receptive language skills) even if their expressive speech is at a less advanced level. By age 5, most children have mastered the rules of grammar and gender and pragmatics—and they are ready to learn the basics of reading and writing.

# Second Language Development

Children who grow up with two or more languages from birth—or shortly thereafter—tend to learn both languages in the same way at the same time. When a child begins developing in one language and a new language is added after about age 3, the second language learning takes a somewhat different path. Most 3-year-olds understand and use a lot of language and understand how language works. Their second language learning is based on that knowledge.

Social and emotional factors influence children's learning of a second language. If a child's first exposure to English coincides with the first day of child care where she is dropped off and left there by her mother for many hours, there's more to consider than just a language difference. Also, preschool and elementary age children might be shy or embarrassed about trying a new language—something that doesn't bother most 12-month-olds.

Research shows that overwhelming young children with a new language does not help them learn it faster. Continuing support for the learning and use of the first language provides a solid foundation that can actually make learning a second language more successful. In order to be effective, that support of the home language must be significant, even if it is not equal to support of the new language. If the child has a lot of language experiences at home with singing, playing, conversations, and reading, then additional home language support at school can be very effective (Espinosa 2010).

> When several refugee families moved to her neighborhood, Rhonda welcomed two 4-year-olds from Somalia into her family child care home. Over the next several months she noticed quite a difference in the language skills of the two children. As she got to know the families, she learned that Ghedi's family engaged in storytelling with Ghedi, but Nadifa's family was not very interested in stories or play and rarely had conversations with their children. Rhonda realized that Nadifa would need to experience more support for her home language while in care. She contacted a local church that helped resettle refugee families and asked for assistance. The church shared some recordings of Somali children's stories and chants, and Rhonda played them for the children during the day. This supported both children's home language skills and allowed Rhonda to learn some Somali words and phrases herself.

Stages of Second Language Development

Home language only

Possible silent period

Actions show understanding

Formulaic speech

Informal language

Academic fluency

## Stages of second language development

Stages of second language development are not attached to any specific ages. The learning process depends on when children start, their skills in the first language, and the quality of support for learning a new language.

**Home language only.** When children enter a new language environment, they may still use their home language for a while. This is to be expected, and an adult who can share even a few words of that home language can foster a positive relationship with children from day one.

**Possible silent period.** Many teachers report experiences with young DLLs who stop talking for a period of time as they observe the new environment and listen to the new language. This may be similar to the experiences of first language development when we think of how much infants learn by observing and listening to language before they say their first word. For many DLLs this is a normal part of their learning process, but we can't predict the length of a typical silent period since it varies from child to child and there may be other developmental and personality variables at work. It is a good idea to keep an eye on a child during this time in case there is another reason for her silence. Is the child playing with the other children in ways that are appropriate for her age? Is she showing signs of depression? Is it possible that the silent period is actually a sign of hearing loss? Don't let six months go by ignoring the child's silence because you think it might be due to the new language. However, if you have investigated the possible causes and found no significant problems, then it may just be this child's way of adjusting to the new language.

**Actions show understanding.** As with young children learning their first language, the brain acquires and catalogs a vast collection of receptive language before it is ready to start producing or saying the words. For some time before they can speak their new language, DLLs will begin to show that they understand by responding to instructions or being able to participate in a game. As careful observers of these behaviors, teachers will be able to document and interpret a child's progress.

> Jean-Marc started kindergarten without seeming to know a word of English, and his school did not have any staff who spoke Haitian Creole. As his teacher tried to help him get used to the new classroom, she noticed that he was first in line whenever she announced recess time. Then she saw Jean-Marc playing a new game that she had just introduced to the children that morning. She could see from his actions that he wasn't ready to speak in English, but he certainly understood a great deal. She became more confident in talking with Jean-Marc using English with lots of visuals and gestures, realizing that he really could understand and learn in the new language.

**Formulaic speech.** This stage is similar, but not identical, to the telegraphic speech stage of first language development. In this stage, older DLLs are able to recognize multiword groups or formulas and use them with some degree of accuracy before they can break down the groups into individual words. For example, Isak learned to say "gimmedat" before he could say the individual words *give*, *me*, and *that*. This early attempt to communicate is not an error—it is a useful way for the brain to begin making sense out of short phrases a child can use to get needs met. Communication is the main focus of the brain's language learning efforts, so this is a good start.

**Informal language.** Many young children have an amazing ability to pick up their new language very quickly. Soon they are talking in sentences, understanding much of what's happening in the classroom, and telling you what they did over the weekend. They may communicate very well in their new language in a year or less. While this progress is important, it represents informal fluency—what we call *playground language*. Within the first six to eight years, much of children's prior learning is coded in their brain in their first language. It's important for teachers to help them build on all of their prior knowledge—learned in English and the home language. Research tells us that children under the age of 6 need continuing support of their home language while they are also developing their second (Espinosa 2010).

**Academic fluency.** Experts believe it may take six or more years for children to develop full academic fluency in the second language to the point that they are ready to do all learning in that language at grade level (Pearson 2008). That means that most children in early childhood settings need ongoing home language practice and experience while they are learning English. Helping children stay in touch with their home language concepts and preliteracy skills seems to allow them to use all of that knowledge plus the new concepts and literacy skills they are learning in English. This powerful combination strengthens children's ability to succeed in school.

# Strategies for Supporting Dual Language Learners

# Getting the Classroom Ready for Dual Language Learners

Five-year-olds Bao and Cam both came to the United States from Vietnam. Bao's family moved to a city and enrolled him in the neighborhood kindergarten. On the first day of school, Bao and his mother nervously entered the building. Bao's mother couldn't read any of the signs explaining where her son was supposed to go, and Bao had never been left in a strange place without his parents before. When they found the room number and opened the door, the teacher seemed surprised to see them. She had not been told that one of the new kindergartners did not speak English. She didn't know what language Bao and his mother were speaking, couldn't pronounce his name, and felt totally unprepared to teach him. Bao's mother looked around and could not find a single familiar word or picture with which to connect. There seemed to be no place for her young son in this school, yet she knew he needed to be there. Finally she pushed him into the classroom and hurried away. She cried. Bao cried. And the teacher felt helpless. She knew from experience that this kind of difficult start to the school year could hinder Bao's learning for months to come.

Cam, on the other hand, moved with his family to a gulf-coast town where there are many Vietnamese families. When his mother brought him to the first day of kindergarten, she saw signs in three languages, including Vietnamese, posted in the building. Thus it was easy for her to figure out where to find Cam's classroom. The English-speaking teacher greeted them with a few words in Vietnamese. She had already posted Cam's name and picture on the attendance sign-in sheet and above his cubby. Cam's mother noticed a display of model Vietnamese fishing boats and saw some children's books in Vietnamese on a shelf in the library area. As she walked out, she heard the teacher singing "Good morning, Cam" in Vietnamese. She smiled. Cam smiled. Later that year, Cam's mother offered to volunteer to welcome other newcomer families to the school. She had such a positive experience that she wanted to help others in the same way.

Getting the classroom ready for dual language learners should begin before the child's first day. In programs that successfully attract, enroll, and maintain good relationships with families of DLLs, every staff member shows respect for diversity and is prepared to welcome and support different languages and cultures. Preparations begin at the program level. Administrators, principals, and directors play an important role in establishing program-wide policies for supporting DLLs and their families. Everyone who works in the program and everyone whose child attends it should be familiar with this policy and work together to implement it.

Teachers devote much attention to setting up a classroom environment to support the learning goals they set for the children. Many factors influence their design choices, including personal tastes and preferences. The set-up of the furnishings can influence children's noise, attention, and activity levels. Teachers may also have to consider guidance from the program or school curriculum, employer policies, limitations imposed by funding, or broader factors such as state or national requirements. Sometimes these factors work against each other, further complicating the planning process.

For example, in a preschool program, you may wish to fill your classroom with soft furnishings, as recommended in the *Early Childhood Environment Rat-*

*ing Scale* (Harms et al. 2005). Soft furnishings can help to reduce background noise and make it easer for DLLs to hear how the teacher pronounces the new words they are learning. In some places, however, local fire or health ordinances prohibit the use of these materials in early childhood classrooms due to allergy or flammability issues.

Federal, state, and local regulations will guide the way your program is established and implemented when you teach DLLs in the early years from birth through third grade. It is important to be familiar with the requirements that affect your program. Working within those guidelines, there are a number of strategies you can use to make young DLLs and their families feel more welcome and supported as they enter your classroom. Here are some suggestions that can enhance your existing classroom environment.

## Teaching staff

To prepare classrooms for DLLs teachers and teaching assistants can use the following suggestions.

◆ Learn information as soon as possible about the home language of each new child. This allows you to prepare a welcoming classroom environment so that the child and the family have the appropriate experiences right from the start.

◆ Add the new languages to functional labels that include phonetic spellings throughout the room.

◆ Contact the public library to borrow books, music, and story CDs in the languages needed.

◆ Find or make puzzles, games, and manipulatives using travel brochures or downloaded photos that will be meaningful for the DLLs in the class. These should represent not only the languages of the new children but also their cultures, interests, and family activities.

◆ Add props such as menus from local ethnic restaurants, empty food packages, and utensils to the pretend play area; offer different kinds of paper in the art area; provide newspapers and magazines in the children's home languages in the literacy area.

◆ Use literature and music in the home languages of DLLs to enhance learning while they are still building English skills. While you might have some English language music or stories that have been translated into other languages, it is also important to have materials that are original or culturally appropriate to the DLL's country of origin.

◆ Establish a strong, predictable classroom routine so DLLs can relax. This helps them know exactly what is going to happen throughout the day, even if they do not understand the verbal or written announcements. Post and refer to a picture schedule to remind them of the order and times of the day's events.

◆ Create name tags and cubby labels with photos of the children. Newcomers will know exactly where they belong and can begin to make connections with the other children, too.

◆ Provide a picture/symbol communication board to help children get their needs met. Include pictures showing the different activities of the day or needs the child may have, such as a drink of water, the bathroom, or a bandage. The board can be an effective communication medium until the teacher and child begin to understand each other's language.

◆ Set up a quiet corner where DLLs can have time to play alone and take a break from the overwhelming demands of a classroom where most people speak a different language. In this way, the environment can serve as an effective stress reliever.

◆ Add a few display items that recognize the language or traditions of the new families. Check items to be sure they would not be considered stereotypes. Don't try to represent an entire culture, but focus on connecting with the things you know about particular families.

## Administrators

Most teachers do not plan the classroom environment completely on their own. Their directors and principals play an important role in supporting them,

> Pablo's family is from Mexico. The family worker at his new child development program learned that his family had lived in a high rise apartment in the city, where his parents worked in the banking industry. Images of Mexican farmers were not culturally familiar for him. The family worker and teachers located photos of the park and playground in Pablo's former city and enlarged them to make posters. They also put out various block accessories that represented city life and buildings.

supervising their efforts, and making sure they have what they need to create a linguistically and culturally appropriate environment. Administrators also control the broader context outside of the classroom. They have to think about the entire organization as well as the image of the program or school in the community.

Here are some suggestions for how directors and principals can help teachers prepare classrooms for DLLs.

◆ Establish and communicate a vision for the program that includes and respects all languages and cultures. Posting a vision statement on the wall is a start, but administrators must also have a clear set of plans and policies to explain how staff should implement the elements of the vision throughout the school or program.

◆ Communicate a respectful message on the program's website and in advertising materials so all families in the community will know they are welcome. This is important for programs that enroll children based on family choice. In the areas where families are required to enroll their children in the local elementary school, the availability of linguistically appropriate information and signs won't influence a parent's choice. Nevertheless, those items do set the stage for a positive attitude about the school. This is where the administrator can lay the foundation for a strong home–school connection.

◆ Offer staff inservice training and ongoing information to support their readiness to meet the needs of DLLs. Professional development should increase diversity awareness and present appropriate practices for teaching DLLs in all learning domains. All teachers should also be familiar with the process of first and second language development as well as literacy development for DLLs. In elementary schools where there may be ESL or bilingual education specialists, it is important that administrators ensure these staff members are not the only adults in the building with the skills needed to support DLLs. General education teachers, therapists, special education teachers, and specialists in physical education, art, music, or computer skills also need professional development. They too must be prepared to adapt their teaching and interaction styles to meet the needs of DLLs.

◆ Ask questions during interviews about job candidates' approach to valuing and addressing diversity during interviews. This will help to identify staff who will respect and support young DLLs and their families. Administrators know that it is not always easy for employees to change their attitudes and practices. Hiring people who are prepared to work effectively with DLLs can help build a united and positive feeling for the entire staff.

◆ Learn which teaching strategies, lesson plans, and classroom set-ups are most appropriate for DLLs. Depending on the age of the child and the type of program, curriculum goals should address both language development and academic content standards, as well as reading, listening, speaking, and writing skills. In the most effective programs from the infant/toddler years to preschool and on to the primary grades, administrators hold high expectations for quality and effectiveness. They know what effective teaching and appropriate materials look like, and they follow through to be sure standards are upheld. To make that possible, administrators need to take care of their own professional learning. Be a role model for continuing professional development and be prepared to help all teachers get what they need to be ready to support DLLs.

◆ Provide the right classroom resources. Teachers depend on program administrators to make sure they have the supplies they need to implement best practices. In multilingual programs this is especially important. The "Ready for Dual Language Learners" Classroom Checklist (see page 35) is intended for use by teachers and administrators. Use it to inform planning and budgeting decisions before the school year starts.

◆ Maintain a collection of classroom resources and materials in different languages. When teachers encounter children who speak new languages, they will have immediate access to appropriate materials.

◆ Support professional learning networks (PLNs) among staff so they can build their language skills and share ideas and activities that have worked with the different languages and cultures represented in their classes. To make PLNs possible, build in sufficient time in teachers' schedules, purchase books or videos teachers can use, hire expert consultants, and arrange visits to model multilingual classrooms.

## Social and family workers

Most early childhood teacher education programs offer coursework on working with families, but this aspect of a teacher's job can still be overwhelming. If your school or program is fortunate enough to have social workers or family workers on staff, you can rely on them as valued partners in your work with young DLLs and their families. Preparing the classroom for DLLs involves more than just placing a few new books on the shelf. Working with other staff can help you get to know each child and prepare to address potential issues or concerns.

Here are some ways social workers and family workers can help prepare classrooms for DLLs.

◆ Get to know incoming families and learn about their languages, traditions, celebrations, activities, music, stories, games, and foods. Many programs use a written home language survey or include questions on enrollment forms. An in-person visit or interview can provide much more information to inform teachers and help them prepare for each new child and family. This is particularly important when caring for infants and toddlers who face both a language barrier and are not yet able to show what they need via actions or gestures.

◆ Work with the classroom teachers to find ways to incorporate some familiar items into the environment that will help the new child and family feel personally welcomed from their first day. For example, if the social worker shares that the new French-Canadian family has a beloved dog, pictures, props, or stories about dogs may help their French-speaking child feel more connected and understood despite initial language barriers. These connections are stronger when they are built on real understanding of the child rather than assumed or generalized cultural images such as hockey posters.

◆ Prepare to connect the family with needed social services or support systems. Many immigrant families are unfamiliar with the family services available in the U.S. With a higher risk for poverty and isolation, families of DLLs may need more active support so they can provide the supportive environment so necessary for their young children to grow up healthy and ready to succeed in school. Research which agencies offer supports in which languages. Try to have on hand some brochures in less common languages.

When any young child starts a new program or school, the first few days are critical. A positive experience can make all the difference in shaping their successful learning within the classroom, the program or school, and the U.S. school system as they progress from grade to grade. Think about how you felt as a young child being left at a strange place for the first time with people you did not know. Or think about your feelings as a parent dropping off your own child at child care program or school for the first time. Coming to a new school is a significant adjustment for any child, but a child who is not familiar with the language, who has just moved from another country, and whose family may be experiencing additional stress is certainly going to face challenges as she adjusts to your program.

A teacher's efforts to ease the transition and make the child feel like an important member of the classroom community will help her adjust more quickly and effectively so she can be an eager and successful learner.

Preparing the classroom is also a way to help you feel ready and confident to smoothly adapt your teaching to meet the needs of young DLLs. When you are well prepared, it is easier to be effective in a diverse classroom. A little advance work before DLLs join your class can help not only their adjustment, but yours as well. Teachers of children from birth though age 8 can use the following checklist to make sure the classroom is well-equipped to provide effective supports for DLLs.

# "Ready for Dual Language Learners" Classroom Checklist

## Language awareness and print materials that children and families notice:

☐ Staff are aware of each child's home language and country of origin and use that knowledge to make the classroom ready for and welcoming to DLLs.

☐ All of the children's languages and cultures are represented in some way in the classroom.

☐ The classroom has a written list and audio recording of a few key welcoming words in each child's language. (This allows school staff and others to use some words in the new child's home language to help him feel at ease.)

☐ There are welcome signs, brochures, and messages on the school website in the different languages used in the community.

☐ Documents for parents are written in simple language, include graphics and pictures to aid understanding, and are translated as needed into families' home languages.

- [ ] Classroom signs and labels are written in different languages (words are accompanied by phonetic spellings so those unfamiliar with the language can pronounce the words when using them in conversations with DLLs) and color coded to help teachers and children distinguish between languages.

- [ ] Classroom labels have clear and appropriate pictures to support meaning.

- [ ] A picture version of the daily schedule is posted on the wall.

- [ ] There are bilingual books, books in home languages, and books with CDs— for every home language in the group.

- [ ] There are plenty of props—puppets, felt pieces, hats, tools, instruments, and such—representing characters, objects, and actions in the stories to enhance children's understanding.

- [ ] Culturally and linguistically appropriate posters and displays (bought, donated, or handmade) are visible.

- [ ] Images, stories, and materials are respectful and free of stereotypes.

- [ ] The outdoor play area has picture and written labels and safety messages in English and the children's home languages.

## Learning center and activity materials that children encounter:

- [ ] Real or realistic materials—dolls, menus, catalogs, clothing, foods and packaging, cooking items, eating utensils, tools—in the dramatic play area represent the children's languages and cultures.

- [ ] Models and pictures of different buildings in the block area represent structures and sights familiar to the children.

- [ ] Art supplies from different cultures (such as Japanese rice paper and calligraphy brushes) are available in the art area.

- [ ] Manipulatives are real and culturally relevant, such as puzzles showing diverse families and familiar items from home, such as socks, for sorting activities.

- ☐ Science exploration materials are familiar and useful instead of fake items or unrealistic representations that have no real use or do not connect to children's knowledge and experiences. For example, children can observe ants in an ant farm.
- ☐ Children eat healthy meals and snacks that incorporate foods familiar to the cultures of all the children in the group. Staff offer optional eating utensils, such as chopsticks.
- ☐ Authentic music from the home countries or in the languages of DLLs is available. Teachers consult families, so that children will recognize selections from their homes as well.
- ☐ The writing center uses writing models and print and handwritten materials (prepared in advance) in the different languages of the children.

## School supports that we teachers can draw on:

- ☐ My school has a clear policy about supporting children with different languages and their families, and the policy is communicated and implemented by all who work in the program.
- ☐ There is a digital camera in the classroom that I can use to take photos of DLLs learning, interacting, and playing during the day. I show photos to parents who may not understand my language, so they know their child is thriving in the program.
- ☐ Staff have access to shared resources stored in a central location so we can save and swap materials in the different home languages of the children in our classrooms.
- ☐ I have posted throughout the room key words in the children's home languages for greeting DLLs, starting conversations, and preventing problems. Other adults and I can use them or we can recognize them when we hear them and respond appropriately.
- ☐ I have access to a picture dictionary, website, or mobile device application that provides translations in the language of every child in the classroom.

- ☐ I have posted a picture/symbol communication board.
- ☐ I have created a lesson-plan form with space to list plans for meeting the needs of DLLs in the classroom.
- ☐ I make available to bilingual staff the guidelines on how and when to use English or their other language with the children.
- ☐ I have access to a digital camera, video camera, or voice recorder to use in recording and tracking the progress of DLL's oral language skills. I save this documentation for assessment, portfolio, and family meetings so that I have a record of children's oral language progress even if I don't understand their words. I have access to help to translate the recording.
- ☐ I have participated in coursework or ongoing professional development to help me refine my strategies for teaching young DLLs.

# Techniques for Teachers Who Speak the Language of the Child

This chapter is unique because it is written as a guide for educators who speak languages other than English in their work with young children. In response to growing diversity in the population of young children, colleges and universities, schools, and child care programs are increasing their efforts to recruit early childhood educators who speak different languages. Hiring staff who speak the languages of the children in the program is a wonderful way to welcome the children and their families. It can enhance program effectiveness when there is always someone available who can speak the different languages as needed. Recent research confirms that this is a positive step, as "teaching reading skills in the first language is more effective in terms of English reading achievement than immersing children in English" (Castro et al. 2011, 266–67).

It is important for educators to build a positive relationship with every child. Each relationship is based on your understanding of the role children's home language and culture play in their self-esteem and in their family's strength. Every teacher and every program selects and plans strategies for teaching DLLs in different ways. They consider the languages spoken by children and the languages spoken by staff, while keeping in mind the curriculum, available resources, and the rules and regulations that govern their work. Educators can adapt the ideas suggested here to their circumstances to fit their needs.

> Marisol is a new assistant in a preschool classroom where more than half of the children speak Spanish. Her new boss, Wyatt, told her that she would serve as a bilingual aide. When she began working in the classroom, she found that the teacher, Susan, used only English when talking with the children. Marisol felt uncomfortable speaking out loud in Spanish. Instead, she whispered in some of the children's ears to interpret what Susan was saying. Sometimes she whispered in Spanish when it was time for the children to sit down so story time could begin. After a while, Susan asked her why she was doing those things. Marisol had to admit she didn't really know. No one had told her exactly what she *should* be doing to make use of her Spanish skills, so she was just trying to be helpful.

An important first step in preparing to teach bilingually is to learn about your state's regulations and guidance on teaching young dual language learners. Each state has requirements for the qualifications and certifications of teachers who provide bilingual education or English as a Second Language programs in kindergarten through third grade. However, teachers of general education from kindergarten through third grade and teachers of infants, toddlers, and preschoolers also are likely to work with DLLs. A report by the federal Office of English Language Acquisition states: "The responsibility for educating ELLs does not lie solely with those teachers who have ESOL or bilingual education licenses, but with all teachers who have or may have ELLs in their classrooms" (Ballantyne et al. 2008, 120). To date only New Jersey and Illinois have clear requirements for bilingual education for preschoolers—and those regulations apply only to programs operated by school districts. In most states, there are no requirements for bilingual teachers or programs for children under the age of 5 years (National Center on Cultural and Linguistic Responsiveness 2012).

Based on developmentally appropriate practice guidance and some strong recent research, you can use the following teaching strategies to teach in two languages with confidence.

## Organization and planning

**Decide when and how you will use each language.** If you teach by yourself, decide during your lesson planning process when you will use English and when you will use your other language. If most of the children speak little or no English, you might start the year speaking the non-English language about 90 percent of the day, then gradually use more English over time. Rules and regulations vary in different settings, but for children in the early years, there is not much research evidence to support increasing the English portion to more than half of the school day.

Keep in mind that bilingual education really does mean teaching in two languages. Most programs and schools expect bilingual teachers to help young children develop English proficiency while also supporting children's progress in their home language. Teaching in the home language helps children learn content and concepts that they might not be ready to comprehend in English. This important foundation will actually support all children's later learning in any language. In addition, young DLLs need clear, consistent exposure to English using natural conversations and responsive, two-way interactions.

Some people believe that young children are like sponges when it comes to learning language. This is not true. Children's brains are certainly primed and ready to focus on key language components like sounds, sequence, tone of voice, rhythm, and patterns, but recognizing these key components takes a lot of systematic exposure to language that refers to the here and now. This exposure should be accomplished in very natural and developmentally appropriate ways—not by drills or rote learning. The key question is, how much of the day will you devote to learning of English and how much time will you teach in your other language? The answer may depend on each individual child's needs and progress, creating excellent opportunities for practicing your skills for differentiated instruction.

If you work with another teacher who speaks English, there may be a few brief instances during the day when you might interpret what she says to a DLL, but this will not be your primary role. Use your own rich language, ideas, creativity, and skills when teaching and interacting with the children. Do collaborative planning with your coteacher to decide how to use each language every day. It is best to follow the classroom curriculum as closely as possible, but you may need to add your own creative touches to help the DLLs learn the content and the context as their classmates do.

**Separate the languages you use.** Some programs, such as dual language immersion programs, designate certain days or weeks during which activities and routines are conducted in the non-English language. Others plan to use the non-English language every afternoon, only at meal times, or during choice time activities. Whatever you plan, try to stick to the language during the designated time period rather than switching back and forth or saying everything in two languages. This use of a single language creates an atmosphere where children can focus on learning one language rather than waiting for the same thing to be said in the other language.

**Keep the children together.** Although you use only one language at a time, there is no need to keep the children separate. If you speak with children only in Hmong and your coteacher speaks only in English, you may find that each of you bonds with the children who speak your language. It is a good thing for DLLs to have an adult they can understand and talk to, but the language difference should not create a divided class. Both teachers should make an extra effort to get to know all of the children and find ways to relate to them. From the infant/toddler years, when each child is assigned a primary caregiver, to elementary classrooms, where there is typically only one teacher, young children need to learn to feel comfortable with a variety of adults who teach and work with them—even if they do not speak the same language. It is a challenging and enriching learning opportunity for young children to spend time with a teacher who speaks a different language. Some school districts use pull-out services to provide ESL supports to DLLs outside of their regular classroom for some period of time. Unfortunately, this practice can make young DLLs feel isolated from their classmates. Supports that are embedded in the regular classroom not only help the young DLL remain a part of the group, but they also make it possible for the general education teacher to observe and learn the strategies used by the ESL specialist.

## Interactions

**Engage in real conversations with the children in their home language.** Ask open-ended questions such as "How do you think the bear in the story felt about losing his friend?" Try to take three or more turns in a conversation using the home language. Remember, it is not just about saying words in the home language. Be sure to pursue children's interests to build on their prior knowledge and increase the depth and breadth of vocabulary and understanding. These rich exchanges and use of the home language are a valuable foundation for children's future as they learn English.

**Repeat often.** The brains of young children depend on repeated exposure to understand and remember new words or ideas. Read the same story every day for a week if the children ask for it, or play the same game over and over again. The ability to differentiate instruction in the elementary grades and to respond to children's abilities and interests in the younger years requires a lot of planning and preparation when working with DLLs. How you use your non-English language effectively will depend on your implementation of developmentally appropriate practices to respond to individual children and the group. There is no one right way to be a bilingual early childhood teacher. The right way is to be flexible enough to change what you do to meet the needs of each child.

**Share your language and culture with all of the children.** Learning about different countries, cultures, traditions, words, foods, and customs is enriching for all children, not just the ones who speak your language. With infants and toddlers, home language interactions may include lullabies, stories, rhymes, songs, and comforting words during caretaking routines. With preschool and kindergarten children, engage in whimsical conversations in the dramatic play area, discuss science observations outdoors, or have social conversations at snack and meal times. These interactions are in addition to the home language songs, games, and stories that are a part of the day already. Elementary classrooms, where the day is more structured, call for using conversational interactions in the context of lessons and planned learning activities. For example, when demonstrating a math concept in the home language, be sure to not only use your non-English language, but to also encourage the children to build their own oral language skills by discussing the lesson with you and each other in that language.

## Activities

**Encourage children to develop rich home language vocabulary.** Build concepts while talking during play or in hands-on learning. Remember that in early childhood, vocabulary is best learned actively and in context. For example, children are more likely to learn the names of different fruits by holding the actual fruits and talking about their properties and how they smell and taste. Passive activities like flashcards, work sheets, or simply listening are not effective teaching strategies for this age group. They are neither developmentally appropriate nor effective. Be a scout for home language materials to enhance your interactions with DLLs. Visit the library or contact local cultural groups and businesses to find books, music, and materials that reflect the children's languages and cultures. You might even contact friends and families in home countries to ask them to send children's books, games, catalogs, pictures, or music for the classroom. If materials are hard to find, try making things yourself using your home language.

It is not necessary—or advisable—to use your language to mirror everything that happens in an English-only class. Learn more about how literacy skills are nurtured and taught in the home countries of the languages in your group. For example, early literacy lessons in the U.S. often focus on rhyming words, but rhyming is not important or relevant in some other languages such as Spanish. Accompany your home language use with culturally appropriate references. Use examples and illustrations from your culture or those of the children. It doesn't work to simply place Spanish letters and words on an English alphabet poster because a banana picture for the letter "b" won't work for *platano*, the Spanish word for banana. Instead of translating what's there, you need to create an alphabet poster that works for the specific language and culture.

## Personal development

**Maintain and enhance your home language skills.** Read a lot of home language materials that interest you. Stay in touch with the language of your profession by reading professional materials like curriculum books or journals to build your adult vocabulary in your home language. If you speak Spanish, read NAEYC's magazine for preschool educators, *Tesoros y Colores*. Establish clear opportunities to meet with and share ideas and materials with other bilingual teachers.

**Work on building and refining your English language skills.** Your home language skills are incredibly valuable in an early childhood classroom, but so are your English skills. If you teach in a bilingual program or school you will do at least some teaching in English. Even if the program is not labeled as bilingual, your supervisor may ask you to help the children begin to learn English as they develop the skills they need to get ready for success in school. When teachers speak in two languages, the quality and accuracy of both languages will be important models for the children.

## Engaging families

**Connect with the parents.** It is important for all of the families—those who are bilingual and those who speak only English—to understand your role and the role of your language in the classroom. Your ability to have meaningful conversations with parents who do not speak English is also an important aspect of your work. Make sure you and your supervisor have a clear understanding about your responsibilities in working with the parents of DLLs. Will you have an informal role in building relationships with them? Or will you be involved in a formal way by interpreting during parent-teacher conferences or special education evaluation meetings? Will you be asked to go on home visits? These tasks vary from one classroom to the next and require careful planning and attention.

**Model home language interactions for families.** Show parents in person or through an online video sharing site how to read, tell stories, and join in playtimes with their children. Create a home language book lending library. Encourage maximum impact by placing the books in a tote bag or backpack with matching puppets and a list of questions families can ask their child. Include instructions for simple parent-child activities to extend children's enjoyment of the book—and learning—at home.

✳     ✳     ✳

These general strategies provide a foundation to help bilingual teaching staff approach their work feeling competent and confident. It is important to work with your supervisor and collaborating teachers to plan more explicitly for daily activities that integrate appropriately with the curriculum. Providing home language support can be part of a general curriculum, a dual language immersion program, or a bilingual program. In any of those settings, the home language supports should be embedded in the chosen curriculum rather than added on as separate activities.

> Marisol attended several workshops on building home language literacy skills in early childhood education settings. She learned some new strategies to bring to the preschool classroom. Her program's curriculum included use of an early literacy program with specially selected story books each week, but the books were available only in English. Marisol worked with Susan to come up with props and actions that would help the Spanish-speaking children understand when she read the book in English. Later in the day, Marisol sat with small groups of children and retold the same story in Spanish, discussing the pictures, characters, and plot with the children. When Susan read the story again the next morning, the Spanish speakers were more confident as they participated in the storytelling. They used their English skills to join in the discussion.

# Techniques for Teachers Who Don't Speak the Language of the Child

This chapter is designed to guide teachers who do not speak the home languages of the children in their class or group. It includes suggestions for supporting DLLs as they learn English as well as information on how to support children's home language skills even if you don't yet speak a word of it. Recent research shows that supporting the home language is a critical component of high-quality early education for DLLs (Castro et al. 2011).

Every teacher, program, and school selects and plans DLL teaching strategies in different ways. They consider the languages spoken by the children and by staff, while keeping in mind the curriculum, available resources, and the rules and regulations that govern their work. Educators can adapt the ideas suggested here to their circumstances. Most importantly, be prepared: learn as much as you can about the children and families so you can plan for language adaptations in advance.

Dana, a new first grade teacher, faces a number of surprises during her first few days as a teacher. She was surprised to learn the number of children in the class who come from families for whom Spanish is their home language. She did not plan to be an ESL teacher and, during her interview, was given the impression that someone else would support the children whose home language is not English. She now realizes that she must find a way to teach these DLLS on her own.

In her first meeting with the principal, Dana mentions the challenges she faces in working with the Spanish-speaking children. "I know that their assessment scores are high enough that they do not qualify for special services, but I see differences in the way they understand words and concepts. I hear them go back and forth between English and Spanish while discussing different topics. I also find it difficult to communicate with their parents who speak very little English." The principal had received some new books on teaching DLLs and shows them to Dana. She also puts her in touch with other teachers, encouraging them to form a school-wide professional learning community to discuss how to apply the teaching strategies suggested in the books.

Usually, the most effective approach combines English language enhancements and supports for the children's home languages. The communication skills children develop in the early childhood years will support their learning in the primary grades and beyond.

## Be prepared

The first step in effectively teaching DLLs is to be prepared. Welcoming diversity into all aspects of the classroom should be part of every early childhood education environment, not just a reaction to enrolling new children who happen to be DLLs. All children should grow up learning to understand and appreciate people who look, sound, or behave differently—and early care and education programs are in a position to help children gain an appreciation for diverse cultures and languages. Teachers can use stories and activities to build understanding of what it means to have a different language and culture.

For infants and toddlers, use board books and picture books that show faces, clothes, and activities of people from different ethnic and cultural backgrounds. These can provide developmentally appropriate opportunities to introduce, display, and discuss images of diversity. Singing songs or learning greetings in a few different languages, including sign language, is also a good way to introduce language diversity. When possible, focus on languages that are present in the neighborhood so children learn words they are likely to use at home and in the community. Learning in two languages does not confuse children, and they will begin to understand that there are sometimes different ways to say the same thing.

Preschoolers often ask questions about why people sound differently or why the color of a friend's skin is not like their own. Use non-fiction texts and picture books with stories that encourage discussions about how we are alike and different. Preschoolers may not yet comprehend where countries are on the map, but they can understand that people from different families make different kinds of food or celebrate different holidays. Getting to know each person in the class is an appropriate goal for a preschooler, rather than learning about broader characteristics of cultures with which they are unfamiliar. It will be more relevant for a 3-year-old to learn that a friend and his family go home to Sweden every summer, where they speak a different language rather than learning about the general cultural practices of some unknown people who live in a foreign country.

School-age children can begin to understand diversity in broader and more practical terms. Posters, books, and music representing different cultures can help children think about diversity outside of their classroom. At this stage, children can learn simple sentences or greetings in languages used in the community so they can talk with people they meet at school and in the neighborhood. Songs can teach children counting or the days of the week in other languages, but there is little a young child can do with that knowledge. Learning to order *ropa vieja* in the local Cuban restaurant would be a more practical approach to language diversity for the early elementary set.

## Support interactions

Teachers can help all the children in the class learn skills to welcome and communicate with newcomers who speak different languages. Be clear about when you are switching from one language to another and model effective communication skills: look at a child who is speaking with you, speak slowly with gestures, and repeat often.

If you work with infants and toddlers you know how often it's necessary to step in to support their interactions with each other, even when they all speak the same language. Helping them to communicate with friends who speak other languages follows the same path. You might highlight the language difference by saying "Oh, Joseph! Your friend said *pelota*! That means *ball* in his language, Spanish. *Pelota*. Can you give Luis the ball? *Aquí*, Luis. *La pelota*! I told Luis he can have the ball." Children under the age of 3 are not likely to understand the concept of translating words from one language to another. However, using just a few words in each child's language helps them learn that their friends understand things in a different way. You can also use this method to make sure both children receive appropriate language input to help them engage in mutual play. Your actions help both children follow along even when you are saying words they don't understand (Nemeth 2012).

Toddlers can learn pragmatic skills that help them to be better communicators. When you teach them to speak slowly, repeat, show what they want, and be gentle and patient when trying to understand others, you are also helping them learn to interact more effectively with their friends who are DLLs. They may need to be reminded often, as you would expect in any toddler group.

Preschool children are able to adapt their language for others who don't easily understand them. You may have heard 3- or 4-year-olds talking baby talk to their younger siblings. They seem to have a natural understanding about emphasizing words, repeating, and changing their tone of voice to make their meaning understood. Capitalize on this natural tendency by turning it into an activity to help children pay more attention to how they use these skills. Use puppets or a flannel board to tell a story about two friends who don't understand each other. Then, involve the children in creating a list of ideas they can use to help the friends get along. Clarify and reinforce these behaviors by commenting when you see any child adapting his or her behavior to help another child understand. "Oh, Sari, I saw you show Min how to put the puzzle together. You used your words and your hands to help him understand!" Patience is also a helpful strategy, but preschoolers will need your help to work on that over time.

School-age children can learn better communication practices by role playing or through pretend play activities. Create a puppet show or story about something the children experienced in the classroom to demonstrate specific communication skills. Be sure to clearly model the desired behaviors yourself whenever possible. Your actions will reinforce the effectiveness of slowing down, emphasizing key words, and patiently repeating when communicating with children who speak different languages. When the children are more successful during interactions with each other, they may come to understand each other better. This leads to greater tolerance and acceptance of classmates despite their differences.

## Use strategies to enhance communication and comprehension

Early childhood teachers with linguistically diverse students tend to have great success when they continue to apply the most effective strategies in their developmentally appropriate toolkit and highlight the ones that focus on building language and communication skills. (Many of the strategies recommended as developmentally appropriate practices are similar to the strategies used by ESL teachers to support language development.)

For example, use visuals to bring your words to life. Concentrate on showing pictures, graphs, and props. Use photos in a book about growing plants to clarify points you are making with children in the science area. Puppets representing different characters can help children understand a storybook plot. Graphs can lend visual supports when talking about math concepts.

Be intentional in your use of gestures, facial expressions, and body language to enhance your meaning. Vary your voice, and use the same silly voice to represent a certain character every time. Use a particular gesture that children will come to understand means that you want them to lower their voices. Many teachers find that adding a few basic sign language signs can help children make connections with oral language as well. When used with spoken words in English, American Sign Language (ASL) signs add visual cues to help children understand and remember your words. The signs are recognizable, predictable gestures that enhance oral communication.

Infants typically go through a period when they focus intently on faces, watching your mouth move as you speak. Make eye contact and encourage that focus when you are speaking in English and when you are speaking in the baby's home language. From about 6 months on, hearing infants benefit from learning key sign language words to support communication (Goodwyn & Acredolo 1993). Many teachers use signs such as *eat, more, milk, sleep, change,* or *bye bye* with infants and toddlers. Use the signs while also speaking the words. The idea is to give children standardized gestures so they can recognize the spoken words that go with them. This is also helpful because the signs bridge language gaps in the classroom. When you say *milk* in Arabic to one child and you use the sign with it, he may recognize the word even if you mispronounce it. The other children will know what you are talking about even when you use a different language.

Many infants learn to use these basic signs before they are ready to say the words in English or in their home language. This helps the children get their needs met and share their interests. It may reduce frustration in the diverse infant/toddler group and seems to support further learning and language development (Goodwyn & Acredolo 1993).

Toddlers can also understand spoken words when teachers carefully use body language and gestures. To make it clear that you are talking about a ball rather than a bowl, hold up the ball while you are talking about it. This is an example of developmentally appropriate practice for any toddler classroom, but it is especially important for DLLs. When talking about bowls or balls, show the visual reminder whether you are using English or the child's home language. It is not necessary to say the word in both languages in the same conversation. If you are interacting with the child using English, then it is best to let the object help him learn the word rather than repeating it in his other language. This will help him make a clear association not only between the English word and the object, but also between the word and the context of conversation that is conducted in English.

Basics of Supporting Dual Language Learners

Preschool children are generally able to understand symbolic representation—they know that pictures represent real things. Teachers can introduce pictures to help children understand words. For example, if a child seems to understand a vocabulary word in the context of a particular book, open the book to show her when you are talking about that same word in a different area. Use body language to further refine communication. Tap your head when you say "put on your hat," or change your voice to a whisper when you are telling the children to be quiet. These strategies can make a big difference in helping young DLLs make sense of the English they hear in the classroom. If you use the same gestures when saying similar things in their home language, the visual connection will help them make the oral language connection, too.

Teachers of DLLs in kindergarten through third grade may have opportunities to work with ESL specialists. This can be a very productive collaboration. To help older children keep up with content learning while they are still building English skills, use a well-known ESL strategy, "supporting comprehensible input." This means that while teaching in English, you also take the time to make sure that DLLs have multiple supports to comprehend what you are saying. For example, don't just say it—demonstrate it, practice it, use hands-on activities to reinforce it, and check for understanding all along the way. Instead of simply telling children how ramps work, have them try different heights, different materials, and different kinds of items to roll up and down the ramps. Have them record their experiences with video or their own sketches, and be sure to interact with individual children as they experiment. This will help you know who understands the concepts and who needs more support. When children are not familiar with English, active explorations help them comprehend not only the concepts in the lesson but also the academic vocabulary.

Another key strategy that goes along with the support of comprehensible input is to emphasize small-group learning and individual interactions. This allows you to maintain eye contact with individual children and help them understand the topics you are covering. Large-group and whole-group lessons are generally counterproductive in any early childhood classroom. They are particularly inappropriate in diverse classrooms because DLLs tend to get overlooked, and teachers are not able to respond to their individual learning needs.

From preschool to third grade, whether implementing your own curriculum or a set curriculum, be sure to differentiate your teaching practices by adjusting activities, materials, and interactions to address individual abilities. This approach is developmentally appropriate for early childhood education in general, and it is very important for DLLs.

## Focus on vocabulary

Intentional teaching of vocabulary is an effective strategy for differentiating instruction. This involves introducing vocabulary in meaningful contexts and uses. In high-quality early childhood education, teachers use activities, explorations, discussions, and stories to emphasize, repeat, and clarify the meanings of words children need to learn and to help them organize key concepts.

Infants and toddlers depend on adults to help them sort out the sounds and meanings of words. You might be most comfortable using English, so when you incorporate words from the children's home languages, pay close attention to the words you use. Emphasize words that the children can use to share their feelings or to get their needs met. Words that describe caretaking activities, self-help skills, meals, and activities are especially useful for infants and toddlers. For example, you might learn the words for *jacket, hat, mittens,* and *shoes* in the children's home languages. Say those words clearly and repeatedly as you help them dress for outdoor play. When telling stories, doing finger plays, or describing the environment only in English, emphasize and repeat those key words as well.

Preschool children benefit from learning more words, as well as more sophisticated words, and the same is true for preschoolers who are DLLs. Once children understand the concept of big versus small, they are ready to learn words like *huge* and *gigantic* if they are accompanied by gestures and emphasis. If a new word such as tiny appears in a story, be sure to use it often in the classroom. Point out a tiny ant or mention that a child only has a tiny bit of waffle left on her plate. Preschoolers do not need vocabulary lessons because the truly intentional teacher can find opportunities for vocabulary building anytime, anywhere. If DLLs are learning important concepts in their home language (such as *grande* and *pequeño*), that knowledge will help them more easily learn the English vocabulary later on.

Once children start primary school, vocabulary demands and expectations increase. While it is true that young children are well-equipped for learning languages, experts caution that they are not sponges. Yes, young children can learn a lot of language from their environment, but ensuring they learn the words and concepts they need to succeed in school takes some planning and attention. When planning activities and lessons, identify key vocabulary words. Provide some of those words in the home languages and use them to introduce topics for DLLs. Also, plan ways to introduce the words in English, to learn what they mean, and to provide different opportunities to practice those words in different ways. This can occur in developmentally appropriate ways, such as when preparing for a field trip to the firehouse. Before the trip introduce the words *fire, truck, hose, ladder, oxygen*, and *hydrant* and highlight the terms in a picture book. After the trip, use those words while children draw pictures of their firehouse experiences.

As the children become more proficient, this explicit support can extend to the structures of the language as well. DLLs need to learn English words and the grammar that supports them. Children may already have a good understanding of sentence structure in their home language, which is a great start, but English has its own set of rules and exceptions to consider. Just as you pay attention to the specific vocabulary words the children need to know, pay attention to the correct phrases and sentences they can use to successfully express their knowledge in English. In the normal course of the school day, look for opportunities to demonstrate and reinforce proper grammar and rules for how we use language. For example, you might need to help a young DLL understand that we say "fire truck" rather than "truck of fire" or "the fire was very hot" rather than "the fire had a lot of hotness."

Even though children may struggle with their use of English, it is important to involve them in discussion, exploration, and conversation in English, rather than leaving them on the sidelines. Use various kinds of questions and words with supports to help them understand. Start with simple questions that can be answered with a word or a nod. As the child gets used to the question-

and-answer process, add questions with choices for answers, and then open-ended questions. Be sure to enhance understanding with visuals.

For infants and toddlers, learn the sign language sign for *where*. Involve the children in seek-and-find games in which you ask "Where is the ball?" or "Where is the sock?" Children who don't understand all the words can use the sign language cue to understand the task and can get involved in the activity. This will also help them learn the words and concepts for ball and sock. Preschool DLLs can participate in discussions when you use predictable questions and ask them in the same way each time. For example, you might do a few activities where you introduce the children to picture symbols for various emotions. When you read a story, always ask a question about how the main character feels, and allow the children to respond verbally and/or by pointing to the pictures. Because you have specifically talked about feelings vocabulary, DLLs are more likely to recognize both the question and the answers in the book discussion. Both of these strategies have also been used successfully to engage school-age DLLs in English only discussions.

## Plan for using English and home languages

It is important to be clear about your plans for when you will use English even if there are some parts of the day or week where children will learn in their home languages. Separate the languages during some activities so that children can focus on trying to learn and use English. You can support their home language at other times.

Some schools and programs serving children from infants through the primary grades implement dual language immersion approaches. These programs assign children to groups so that half speak one language and half speak another, such as English and Mandarin. The class has either one bilingual teacher, or two teachers, one who speaks English and one who speaks Mandarin. Children spend half of the time learning in English and half in Mandarin. As a result, all of the children have some home language learning and some learning in the other language. They all learn both languages. Some programs split the languages between morning and afternoon, or every other day, or they may switch languages each week. Preliminary research (Barnett et al. 2007) shows promising results with this type of program, and it highlights the value of keeping the languages clear and separate for the children.

As with all young children, DLLs need supports built into their learning experiences to help them make connections between words and concepts and between sounds and words. When DLLs face the additional challenge of learning in a new language, teachers must enhance these supports. Give DLLs plenty of time to repeat activities over time and in different contexts, so they have more examples to help them gain deeper understanding of vocabulary and meaning. Use familiar items that help them build on prior knowledge.

Dana read her first book on teaching strategies for DLLs and then met with the new professional learning network (PLN) group to discuss how to put ideas into action. Together they agreed that they were spending too much time working with DLLs who looked puzzled or who sat passively when the teacher tried to teach sorting with plain plastic shapes. They decided to bring in familiar items from home, such as socks or food packages with recipes on the back, and use them for more functional and realistic math activities. At their next meeting, everyone in the PLN group reported that the activity succeeded. Dana explained that she saw DLLs respond brightly to items they understood and they immediately set about sorting them without even being told. The group then brainstormed about other real items they could use to teach all kinds of concepts.

Finally, there has to be time in each day when young DLLs have opportunities to play, work, and learn in their home language. How that happens will differ from classroom to classroom. Even if you do not yet speak each child's home language, it is important to show support and build your relationship with DLLs by learning at least a few key words. Ask parents, colleagues, or community volunteers for help, or you might try online translation programs.

You can add to home language supports by stocking your classroom with materials that the children can use or that can help you pronounce the words in the children's languages. Ask your library about resources they provide in other languages such as books with CDs, music, computer activities, or DVDs. Not only can the child spend some time each day with these language supports, but you may find they help you learn useful words and phrases that really work to support young DLLs. Seek volunteers who can read, sing, or play with children in their home languages.

Children's families are the most valuable partners you will have in your efforts to support home languages for DLLs. Offer books and activities families can use to support their child's literacy development in the home language to extend learning at home. Communicate regularly about topics children are exploring at school so parents can talk about them at home. Ask parents to visit the classroom or to record books and songs to send in for their children to enjoy during the day. You can provide the books and the recording equipment.

To ensure families are effective partners in the home language learning process, plan to do more than provide resources and information. Make an extra effort to show parents how to read and discuss stories or how to tell stories from memory or from wordless books. Invite them in to see how you read to the children, or provide a video showing parents exploring the neighborhood and having fun conversations. Invite them to a family cooking night or a Fun with Science workshop together with their children. While they are there, demonstrate how you have significant conversations with individual children. Parents don't always know how important all this talking with young children can be, but they do want what's best for their children, and that's a great foundation for a partnership.

Dana realized that she needed as much support as she could get to teach DLLs effectively. As she had told her principal, working with families was one of her biggest challenges. Together, they thought about ways to make more information accessible to parents in their home languages, including contacting neighboring school districts to share resources and materials in the languages needed for Dana's class. Dana focused on learning more Spanish words and phrases, and she invited a colleague to help interpret during her conversations with parents. She was able to get parents more involved in daily classroom activities and they were more confident in supporting children as they did their homework. With this enhanced relationship with the parents, Dana found that the DLLs seemed to be thriving too.

# Supporting Preservice and Inservice Teachers of Young DLLs

Marisol is a newly hired bilingual teaching assistant. Her supervisor, Wyatt, does not speak any Spanish. After the first week of school, Wyatt asked Marisol how she was doing. Marisol said she didn't know how she was doing because she didn't know what to do. At the close of their conversation, they identified useful training opportunities for Marisol. After attending the workshops and trying the new strategies, she explained them to Wyatt. Together, they can come up with new resources or solutions to problems that Marisol encounters.

Factors that make early childhood teachers successful include the teachers' own motivation and disposition, the preparation they have before starting the job (preservice training), and the support and professional development received while they work as teachers (inservice training and supervision). Teachers are not likely to improve their ability to work effectively with children who speak different languages or who come from different cultures by reading a single book or attending one workshop on the topic. In a report for the Center for American Progress, Samson and Collins (2012) found that teachers in the United States are not regularly exposed to strong coursework on teaching DLLs. They make a critical point: "the reality is that most, if not all teachers have or can expect to have ELL students in their classroom and therefore must be prepared to support these children" (1–2).

## Preservice preparation

Teacher preparation programs at colleges and universities have a responsibility to offer a curriculum that addresses the changing circumstances and needs of children and families in the United States. Traditionally, higher education has provided separate programs for English as a second language (ESL), bilingual education, special education, and elementary or early childhood general education. If you are a student in one of these programs, you can benefit from learning more about the topics addressed in the other programs. A well-rounded early childhood teacher should know about general education, special education, ESL, and bilingual education. Early childhood education settings do not always place children in classrooms according to these specific categories. Many early childhood educators work in inclusion programs where children speak different languages and have a wide range of abilities. Others work with children who have diverse needs and abilities because the children have not yet been assessed and identified for placement in specialized programs or services.

This is an important consideration for college professors, advisors, or practicum supervisors. Some colleges do provide a collaborative cross-disciplinary approach to early childhood teacher preparation. Others could do more in this area to ensure that teacher candidates have preservice learning experiences in all areas that will likely be part of their jobs after they graduate. This is not simply a question of requiring teacher candidates to take a sampling of isolated courses on special education methods, ESL strategies, or bilingual education practices. Ideally, a preservice teacher should experience coursework and practice teaching that blend the disciplines and directly address how they work together. Teachers not only need to know techniques for supporting DLLs and strategies for teaching children with identified disabilities; they also should know how to teach children with special needs who speak a non-English language at home. Some programs offer or require teacher candidates to take one or more courses in ESL practices, but a disconnect remains because those courses rarely address the learning needs of children below first grade. Preservice teachers also need to learn developmentally appropriate applications of teaching strategies they study in other disciplines so they are suitable for use with children in preK through third grade.

Now more than ever, all early childhood teacher education programs must prepare candidates to work with DLLs using age-appropriate methods that support children with widely diverse needs. Three critical themes should be covered by specific coursework as well as through enhancements to existing early childhood education courses:

◆ The development of first and second languages in children from birth through age 8

◆ Strategies for teaching DLLs, including different techniques that bilingual teachers and teachers who do not speak the languages of the children in their classes can use

◆ Cultural awareness and culturally responsive communication

In their summary of recent findings, Samson and Collins (2012) conclude that teachers need to understand how the brain develops language and know the similarities and differences in the way children learn first and second languages. They urge preservice teacher education programs to provide significant coursework to help teachers enter the field with a strong understanding of the importance of oral language development in both the home language and English. Further, they suggest that teachers learn how to intentionally teach academic vocabulary, such as *magnet, graph, cooperate, illustrate, sink, float, repeat,* and *relax*. These specialized words help children understand academic content in school. Samson and Collins' recommendations extend to the understanding of the cultural context of children's language learning. Since colleges and universities generally can't be expected to add another year onto their teacher education programs, these topics must be covered within existing course requirements.

Colleges and universities, particularly those in regions with highly diverse populations, are working hard to recruit bilingual teacher candidates and to provide learning experiences that realistically reflect the kinds of teaching positions they will have. Some teacher candidates pursue a certificate or endorsement in bilingual education. This credential is usually not required—or even available—for those who teach infants, toddlers, or preschoolers. Still, bilingual students are entering teacher preparation programs in unprecedented numbers (Bireda & Chait 2011). They need to learn developmentally appropriate strategies for using their language assets to support learning in early childhood classrooms. Course instructors can use this book to prepare future teachers who are bilingual to intentionally implement language support techniques with young DLLs. If you are an instructor who supervises teachers in practicum placements, you will support their work in both of their languages. You will also need to work more closely with cooperating schools where your practicum students are placed to ensure that the learning environment offers positive and constructive experiences for bilingual teacher candidates.

## Inservice support

Administrators and directors can support teachers of DLLs by learning more about effective strategies for working with these children and families. Research professional development opportunities for you and your staff. Make sure the staff library is stocked with books, journals, and videos on strategies for teaching dual language learners. Share the techniques in this book with staff, and suggest ways to adapt them so they are effective for the children and families in your school or program.

You won't have to start or add a new curriculum model for DLLs; staff can modify the strategies in this book to fit the established curricula. Preparing language adaptations does require significant time. To support teachers' high-quality implementation, administrators can allow for required planning time. You can support effective services for DLLs by acquiring linguistically and culturally appropriate materials for the classrooms. The best outcomes are likely when administrators, teachers, and families work together toward a better and more responsive approach to linguistic diversity in the early childhood program.

## How to support the monolingual staff

Here are some inservice professional development suggestions to help administrators support their monolingual staff in teaching DLLs effectively.

**Stay informed about new policies, research, and expert guidance.** Lead staff toward the goal of providing the best possible level of high-quality teaching practices in diverse environments. Bring in professional development specialists, and be sure you participate in the sessions as well. This increases your knowledge base, allows you to set expectations for staff, and enables you to support them in meeting their goals.

**Provide resources and time to help staff learn children's home languages.** Encourage them to use these languages not only for teaching, but also to build relationships with children and families.

**Encourage teachers to use nonverbal language supports and visual cues in all their teaching.** When this becomes intentional and systematic, teaching is more accessible and comprehensible to all children, especially DLLs. Share ideas and resources for culturally and linguistically relevant classroom displays, provide a budget for purchasing props and learning materials, and offer classes for teachers on making visual supports or enhancing their nonverbal communications skills.

**Collect classroom resources to support the different languages in your early childhood setting.** Have bilingual books in different languages, music CDs, digital content such as computer software or mobile apps, and multilingual activity kits readily available in a central library. Teachers will not waste time searching for the same things over and over.

**Build relationships with members of the community who represent the languages and cultures found in your setting.** Direct teachers to these human resources who might help by volunteering in the classroom, finding linguistically and culturally authentic materials, or answering questions about language or cultural practices.

**Provide opportunities for teachers to learn and plan together.** As a team, teachers can develop strategies that will meet the needs of the particular population of DLLs in their classrooms at any given time.

**Find out what teachers already know, what they want to know, and what they need to know about teaching young DLLs.** Respond with formal and informal individualized professional development. In addition to workshops led by expert presenters, consider webinars or idea sharing via social media on forums in Twitter, LinkedIn, Facebook, or other online groups.

**Be a model professional learner and leader for your staff.** Professional development is most effective when valued and recognized by administrators. When staff learn new strategies, look for them when observing classes and reinforce them through staff meeting discussions.

## How to support the bilingual staff

Recruiting bilingual teachers and assistants to meet the language needs of children and families is an important step, but not the only one to take. Just because teachers or assistants are bilingual does not mean they know how to use their languages in the classroom. They might require targeted professional development to learn effective strategies and how to balance the use of the two languages. It is the employer's responsibility to provide orientation and ongoing support to newly hired bilingual staff so they can make the best use of their languages in their work. Directors and principals who employ bilingual staff must have a clear understanding of how each teacher's language skills can best benefit the children and have a plan for making the best use of these skills. Here are some suggestions for that plan.

**Ask many questions in the interview.** Teachers who are being hired to offer bilingual education services in a school district will need to pass language fluency tests in English and the language of instruction, according to Title III regulations. When hiring bilingual staff, you will want to learn more about the candidate's language experiences. Educators who grew up in a bilingual environment might be fluent in both languages, but it is important to learn if their non-English language skills include the kinds of talking and writing that will help them be an effective bilingual early childhood teacher. Inquire about the candidates' experience teaching in their home language. Ask about their level of education in their home language. Did they learn to read and write in their home language in school in another country or did they learn informally after moving to the U.S.? Did they participate in training or coursework related to early childhood education in their home language? You will also want to know what they currently do to keep up with the growth and sophistication of their language (e.g., do they read for recreation or for professional development in their home language?).

It is important to remember that being able to speak another language is a valuable asset, but not all people who are bilingual have learned that language in the same way or have the same skills. Do not assume a bilingual staff member is capable of translating information or conducting training in their non-English language. Be sure to ask whether a candidate has experience translating written documents or serving as an interpreter during conversations or meetings.

**Create a language policy.** It's important for all staff to know when and how you expect or encourage the use of non-English languages in the early childhood setting. Parents and English-speaking staff also must understand your expectations of bilingual staff so everyone can work together effectively. Some points to consider when developing this policy are

◆ How and when will bilingual teachers use their home language, and how and when will they use English?

◆ What is the role of bilingual teachers in working with the families of DLLs?

◆ What is the role of bilingual teachers in helping with assessment?

◆ What is the role of bilingual teachers in helping other teachers with their DLLs in other classrooms?

◆ What is the role of bilingual teachers in providing translations or interpreting for families?

**Provide an orientation.** In addition to a standard staff orientation, prepare bilingual staff by sharing specific guidance and classroom strategies for supporting children's learning. Turn your language policy into a guidebook.

**Support the work of bilingual staff.** You may not always understand the language they use, but you can still provide what they need to be effective educators. Work with other bilingual coaches, mentors, and colleagues to learn new ways to observe and provide feedback to bilingual staff.

**Support ongoing professional development.** If you hired bilingual staff because you value their language skills, then you will want to support their continuing growth and learning about language development as well as strategies for supporting children's home languages and English development. When possible, provide professional development materials in their home languages. Also, think about encouraging bilingual teachers to work with English-speaking teachers so they can help each other practice in the other language.

## How to support bilingual volunteers

Bilingual volunteers can be a wonderful asset when introducing home language learning in your setting. Volunteers bring their own talents, interests, cultural knowledge, and experiences to their work with children. Enlisting volunteers is especially effective when you cannot find qualified staff who speak all the languages spoken by children and families.

For bilingual volunteers to have the most positive impact on children's learning, they need to know how to support that learning appropriately. Before they start working in the classroom, meet with them, provide a brief orientation, and prepare and distribute copies of written guidelines. For example, share some pointers on reading aloud to young children, talk about the value of having interesting give-and-take conversations, and encourage use of their home language even when English speakers are part of the activity.

> Ana, a toddler teacher, invited Mr. Lee to visit his granddaughter's classroom once a week. A wonderfully talented musician, Mr. Lee brought traditional Chinese songs and instruments to share with the children. Before his first visit, Ana met with him over coffee to talk about what he would be doing with the group. She explained that she hoped the children could learn some of the Chinese language. They talked about how he could use songs and how to enhance their learning potential. He would talk about the song first, sing it with motions, and after the children had learned the song he would ask them questions—all in Chinese. She noted that toddlers need to hear a lot of repetition, and it was perfectly fine if he found himself singing the same songs with them week after week.

## Special notes for coaches and supervisors

You might wonder how it is possible to supervise and support a staff member who uses a language you don't understand. This is certainly a valid concern. It will be worth the effort to learn some new coaching and supervision strategies that will work with your bilingual staff. With the strategies listed here, you will find that it is possible to provide effective coaching and supervision for teachers who use other languages in their classroom practice.

**Look for signs of rich, engaging interactions between a bilingual teacher and one or more children.** Such signs include intense concentration, lots of expression in tone of voice, and descriptive hand gestures on the part of the teacher and child. You may not understand the words, but you will be able to see that meaningful learning is taking place.

**Look for evidence that the interactions have a positive and nurturing tone.** Nonverbal cues such as gentle touch, a smiling teacher and child, shared interest or activity, and enthusiasm can reveal a lot about the conversation.

**Watch for the number of times the turns go back and forth in conversations.** Even if you do not understand what is being said, you can learn a lot about the interaction. For example, if you observe that the teacher says something and the child answers with just one word and then both adult and child turn away from each other, you will realize that further coaching and professional development may be needed, so the teacher can learn strategies for fully engaging children in conversation and learning.

**Support different language professional learning communities (PLCs).** Provide resources in those languages. For example, you might order subscriptions to *Tesoros y Colores*, the Spanish version of NAEYC's magazine *Teaching Young Children*. Set aside some time for the Spanish-speaking staff to read and discuss an article in Spanish. Be sure to include the English speakers on your staff who want to learn Spanish as well. This kind of professional development sends the message that you may not understand Spanish, but you greatly value it and want the Spanish used in your classrooms to be proper, correct, and include lots of variety.

**Reach out to the larger community to trade services with colleagues who speak the languages you need.** Many supervisors look within their own walls and lament that they have no one who can help them observe in multilingual classrooms. Learn what language resources are available in neighboring towns and districts. Perhaps you and a colleague can observe in each other's classrooms so staff can get feedback from someone who understands their non-English language. If necessary, you might record video clips to discuss with bilingual colleagues if they can't visit the classrooms when school is in session.

**Ask bilingual staff to provide their own account of what they are trying to accomplish with their language use in the classroom.** Discuss ways to improve practice and achieve goals. As with any other kind of supervision, self-reflection is a vital component of the cycle of improvement.

**Maintain appropriate expectations for bilingual staff members.** If the curriculum materials are all in English, can you purchase language-appropriate materials? If you need your bilingual teachers to adapt and translate materials, you should consider giving them the time and compensation that would match this added responsibility. Connect bilingual staff from different grades or buildings so they can share the work, making things feasible and more effective for all.

*     *     *

Dual language learners deserve the best early childhood education possible—as do all young children. Meeting the needs of young DLLs and helping them achieve positive educational outcomes presents a number of challenges. Administrators can make it possible to meet those challenges when they have appropriate expectations, ensure that classrooms are properly equipped, and provide ongoing support for all staff.

This book began by stating that dual language learners make up nearly 25 percent of our population of young children, and their needs must be addressed. No classroom, school, district, or state can consider their educational efforts successful if they fail to meet the needs of a quarter of their students. However, 25 percent is not the most important number to consider. Excellence in early childhood education starts with your work—one child at a time.

# Frequently Asked Questions

# Frequently Asked Questions

## 1. Why should I support the home language of a dual language learner when I only speak English?

There are four main reasons why young children need support for their home language when they are in early childhood settings.

◆ Recent research shows that support for early development of, and learning in, the home language leads to later success in learning English.

◆ Children's home language is part of their identity. Respecting and giving attention to it encourages children's self-esteem.

◆ The home language connects children with their parents and grandparents, thereby helping strengthen family bonds.

◆ Support for children's home language helps them fit in socially and helps all children to grow up in an environment of mutual respect and acceptance.

For more on this topic, see the chapter "Understanding the Value of Supporting the Home Language" in Part I.

## 2. How can I encourage the children to communicate and play together in a multilingual group?

You can explicitly teach all children to interact successfully across potential language barriers in several ways. Here are some suggestions:

◆ Demonstrate skills that help children communicate with someone who speaks another language. For example, speak slowly, repeat often, and use gestures while demonstrating what they mean.

◆ Pair children with different home languages and then provide opportunities for them to do chores and play together so they can get to know and help each other.

◆ Play cooperative games that encourage working and having fun together. Children can paint a mural, plant a garden, or play a game where everyone has to find something red and put it on the table before the song ends. These games encourage children to help each other and learn the value of each other's friendship, despite language differences.

◆ Play and dance to music in children's home languages and in English.

## 3. All the teachers in my program speak only English. How can we find ways to support home languages?

Part I of this book answers this in detail. Here are a few ideas you can try. Teachers can model their willingness to learn children's languages and show children that their language differences do not keep them apart. Use bilingual storybooks or CDs from your classroom library to learn a few useful words and phrases in the children's home languages. Start with a few key words you can use with children during the day. Then, find opportunities to practice with supportive friends and colleagues. Share family-style meals during which adults and children participate in conversations in the non-English language. It's best to not have music playing in the background, which could be distracting. Focus on social interactions and enjoying quality time together. Ask some parents to help you add labels around the room in the languages spoken by the children.

Ask them to spell the words phonetically so you can pronounce and use the words in conversations throughout the room. You may be surprised at how quickly you can learn new languages when you take it one step at a time.

## 4. I teach a dual language immersion kindergarten class where half of the children speak English and half speak Mandarin Chinese. The program is divided so that all children spend some time each week learning in English and some time in Mandarin. How can I encourage parents to support the language that is new to them and their children?

Parents can get bilingual story books with CDs or bilingual e-book apps to use on an MP3 player or tablet. Familiar music or games with Chinese and English words also help reinforce language learning. Suggest they try watching television programs or children's movies in the unfamiliar language that are subtitled in the home language. These familiar items will make it easier for families to learn some of the new language along with their child. Send home materials they can use to extend learning at home. When families are aware of the games the class plays, songs they sing, or stories they read, they will be able to encourage their child to tell them about her day. The child will feel the power of learning a new language she can share with her family.

## 5. What kinds of support can I offer when the child speaks a heritage language (such as an indigenous Indian language with strong cultural connections but little or no written system) and so examples can't be found at the local book or music store?

A heritage language, like all home languages, is part of who a person is, and it is an important source of family strength and social belonging. It is important to respect what each child brings to school, no matter how challenging it is to do so. It may be harder to find materials in some languages, but teachers can enlist the help of parents. Ask them to record stories or songs that can be shared in the classroom. Seek community volunteers to create culturally relevant materials for the classroom, even if the language itself cannot be written down. Story-telling and cooking are two activities that work well for passing down words, thoughts, and cultural traditions. Invite family members to visit the class and participate in these activities during the day.

## 6. A few children in my class who are DLLs seem reluctant to speak. Should I force them so they can practice?

Children learning a second language in preschool and elementary school have a lot more to worry about than they would if they were infants learning their first language. The language learning process is complicated by a number of factors, such as the child's previous experiences, temperament, social confidence, at-titudes about language, and the way he is treated by peers and adults. The most effective strategies for including DLLs depend on getting to know each child as an individual and developing techniques that will work best with that child. Here are some examples:

◆ If a child doesn't like to be singled out in front of a group, have more indi-vidual interactions.

◆ For children who don't like to be called on to talk in front of others, it often helps to invite them to participate in choral speaking. For example, read a story in English that has predictable responses, like *The Three Little Pigs*. When it's time to participate, have all children say the wolf's huff-and-puff part together.

◆ To help children practice oral language skills without being embarrassed, sing songs together.

◆ Create a quiet corner where a DLL can go to play or read quietly for a little break from the stress of trying to participate in so much language learning.

Over time, these supportive strategies can encourage children to feel more comfortable using their new language at school. At the same time, it is impor-tant to show them that their attempts to communicate and participate using their home language are valued. Honor children's language abilities by introducing bilingual books and games, watching videos, and reading about life in the different countries where the child's language is spoken. Invite volunteers who speak a child's home language to come to your classroom.

## 7. I work with infants. Does it really matter what language I use, since they don't talk yet?

It matters very much what language you use. Infants' brains are very well equipped to learn one or more languages, so much of their early experiences are already being organized in their brains in their home language. Building on those learning experiences and language development can be critical to helping children learn new things while in your care. Be very clear about when you choose to support the home language and when you choose to teach in English, so the child has contextual cues to learn the separate languages. For example, you might use the home language during diaper changes but read stories in English. Connecting with their home language may also help children feel more comfortable in their caregiving environment. It is also a good idea to introduce infants to high-quality language experiences in English so they can continue learning in both languages throughout the early years.

## 8. Do children adopted from another country still need support for their home language?

There is a growing body of research about international adoptions. The age of the child at the time of the adoption is very important in making plans for supporting their home language and English learning. The answer might be different if the child were adopted at the age of 6 months, when her experience with her first language is not very deep and she is more likely to be able to leave it behind with few consequences. A 2½-year-old child, however, has already learned much in the home language.

We know in an ideal world that supporting the home language would be the best approach. However, when a child is adopted by a monolingual English-speaking family and has no access to the home language in the neighborhood or community, then it is likely that her home language will fade out. Maintaining language skills depends on active and productive conversation. Offering a few songs or stories in preschool is a good way to celebrate the child's first culture but is not likely to give her the conversational practice she really needs to maintain her language skills. Discuss the situation with the family and find out how they want the program to address their child's language and culture in the classroom.

There is a helpful chapter on this topic in *Dual Language Development and Disorders*, by Johanne Paradis, Fred Genesee, and Martha B. Crago.

## 9. Some parents say they do not want their child to speak or learn in their home language at school. They want their child to use only English. Do I have to follow their wishes?

Let parents know that you share their goal of helping their child to learn English and preparing him for success in school and in life. Express that, as an educator, you know that the best way to achieve that goal is to continue supporting the home language during the early years. Being respectful does not mean agreeing with everything parents say. Out of respect for the family, it is important to share your knowledge and expertise when necessary. You might explain that rushing into English while young children are still in the process of learning their home language may cause them to miss out on important concepts and experiences that form the basis for language development. In addition, note that each child's home language is part of who they are, and it is the glue that strengthens family bonds. Strong sense of self and strong family support are two key factors in school readiness and success.

## 10. My school has several bilingual teaching assistants who support the children's home languages. How should they be using their languages in the classroom?

The chapter "Techniques for Teachers Who Speak the Language of the Child" in Part II offers strategies for bilingual educators on how to use their language assets in the classroom. The most important point is that the non-English language should be used to enrich and enliven the DLLs' learning experiences, not just for classroom management. Staff who are lucky enough to speak multiple languages need to use interesting, descriptive, responsive, and correct language when speaking with young DLLs.

# References

Ballantyne, K.G., A.R. Sanderman & J. Levy. 2008. Educating English language learners: Building teacher capacity. Washington, DC: National Clearinghouse for English Language Acquisition. Online: www.ncela.gwu.edu/files/uploads/3/EducatingELLs-BuildingTeacherCapacityVol3.pdf.

Barnett, W.S., D.J. Yarosz, J. Thomas, K. Jung & D. Blanco. 2007. Two-way and monolingual immersion in preschool education: An experimental comparison. *Early Childhood Research Quarterly* 22 (3): 277–93.

Bialystok, E., & M.M. Martin. 2004. Attention and inhibition in bilingual children: Evidence from the dimensional change card sort task. *Developmental Science* 7 (3): 325–39.

Bireda, S., & R. Chait. 2011. Increasing teacher diversity: Strategies to improve the teacher workforce. Washington, DC: Center for American Progress. Online: www.americanprogress.org/issues/2011/11/pdf/chait_diversity.pdf.

Castro, D.C., L.M. Espinosa & M.M. Páez. 2011. Defining and measuring quality in early childhood practices that promote dual language learners' development and learning. In *Quality measurement in early childhood settings*, eds. M. Zaslow, I. Martinez-Beck, K. Tout & T. Halle, 257–80. Baltimore, MD: Paul H. Brookes.

Espinosa, L.M. 2010. *Getting it RIGHT for young children from diverse backgrounds: Applying research to improve practice.* Upper Saddle River, NJ: Pearson.

Genesee, F. 2008. Early dual language learning. *Zero to Three* 29 (1): 17–23.

Genesee, F., & P. Gandara. 1999. Bilingual education programs: A cross-national perspective. *Journal of Social Issues* 55 (4): 665–85.

Goodwyn, S.W., & L.P. Acredolo. 1993. Symbolic gesture versus word: Is there a modality advantage for onset of symbol use? *Child Development* 64 (3): 688–701.

Gottardo, A., & A. Grant. 2008. Defining bilingualism. *Encyclopedia of Language and Literacy Development* (1–7). London, ON: Canadian Language and Literacy Research Network. Online: www.literacyencyclopedia.ca/pdfs/Defining_Bilingualism.pdf.

Han, W.J. 2012. Bilingualism and academic achievement. *Child Development* 83 (1): 300–21.

Harms, T., R.M. Clifford & D. Cryer. 2005. *Early childhood environment rating scale.* Rev. ed. New York: Teachers College Press.

Kuhl, P. 2010. The linguistic genius of babies. Filmed October 2010. TED video, 10:18. Posted February 2011. Online: www.ted.com/talks/patricia_kuhl_the_linguistic_genius_of_babies.html.

National Center on Cultural and Linguistic Responsiveness. 2012. Dual language learners in state early learning guidelines and standards. Washington, DC: Author. Online: http://eclkc.ohs.acf.hhs.gov/hslc/tta-system/cultural-linguistic/center/state-guidelines/dll_guidelines.html.

Nemeth, K.N. 2012. *Many languages, building connections: Supporting infants and toddlers who are dual language learners.* Lewisville, NC: Gryphon House.

Pearson, B.Z. 2008. *Raising a bilingual child: a step-by-step guide for parents.* New York: Random House.

Paradis, J., F. Genesee & M.B. Crago. 2011. *Dual language development and disorders: A handbook of bilingualism and second language learning.* 2d ed. Baltimore, MD: Paul H. Brookes.

Samson, J.F., & B.A. Collins. 2012. Preparing all teachers to meet the needs of English language learners: Applying research to policy and practice for teacher effectiveness. Washington, DC: Center for American Progress. Online: www.americanprogress.org/issues/2012/04/teachers_ell.html.

Wong Fillmore, L. 1991. When learning a second language means losing the first. *Early Childhood Research Quarterly* 6 (3): 323–46.

# Resources

## Print

Barnett, W.S., D.J. Yarosz, J. Thomas, K. Jung & D. Blanco. 2007. Two-way and monolingual immersion in preschool education: An experimental comparison. *Early Childhood Research Quarterly* 22 (3): 277–93.

Castro, D.C., L.M. Espinosa & M.M. Páez. 2011. Defining and measuring quality in early childhood practices that promote dual language learners' development and learning. In *Quality measurement in early childhood settings*, eds. M. Zaslow, I. Martinez-Beck, K. Tout & T. Halle, 257–80. Baltimore, MD: Paul H. Brookes.

Chen, J.J., & S.H. Shire. 2011. Strategic teaching: Fostering communication skills in diverse young learners. *Young Children* 66 (2): 20–27.

Derman-Sparks, D., & J.O. Edwards. 2010. *Anti-bias education for young children and ourselves*. Washington, DC: NAEYC.

Dragan, P.B. 2005. *A how-to guide for teaching English language learners in the primary classroom*. Portsmouth, NH: Heinemann.

Espinosa, L.M. 2010. *Getting it right for young children from diverse backgrounds: Applying research to improve practice*. Upper Saddle River, NJ: Pearson.

Genesee, F. 2008. Early dual language learning. *Zero to Three* 29 (1): 17–23.

Genishi, C., & A.H. Dyson. 2009. *Children, language and literacy: Diverse learners in diverse times*. New York: Teachers College Press; Washington, DC: NAEYC.

Gillanders, C., & D.C. Castro. 2011. Storybook reading for young dual language learners. *Young Children* 66 (1): 91–95.

Han, W.J. 2012. Bilingualism and academic achievement. *Child Development* 83 (1): 300–21.

Howes, C., J.T. Downer & R.C. Pianta, eds. 2011. *Dual language learners in the early childhood classroom.* Baltimore, MD: Paul H. Brookes.

Meier, D.R. 2004. *The young child's memory for words: Developing first and second language and literacy.* New York: Teachers College Press.

Nemeth, K.N. 2009. *Many languages, one classroom: Teaching dual and English language learners.* Beltsville, MD: Gryphon House.

Nemeth, K. 2009. Meeting the home language mandate: Practical strategies for all classrooms. *Young Children* 64 (2): 36–39, 41–42.

Nemeth, K.N. 2012. *Many languages, building connections: Supporting infants and toddlers who are dual language learners.* Lewisville, NC: Gryphon House.

Nemeth, K., & P. Brillante. 2011. Solving the puzzle: Dual language learners with challenging behaviors. *Young Children* 66 (4): 12–17.

Paradis, J., F. Genesee & M.B. Crago. 2011. *Dual language development and disorders: A handbook of bilingualism and second language learning.* 2d ed. Baltimore, MD: Paul H. Brookes.

Tabors, P.O. 2008. *One child, two languages: A guide for early childhood educators of children learning English as a second language.* Baltimore, MD: Paul H. Brookes.

Youngquist, J., & B. Martínez-Griego. 2009. Learning in English, learning in Spanish: A Head Start program changes its approach. *Young Children* 64 (4): 92–99.

## Websites

Colorín Colorado. The bilingual literacy (Spanish and English) website of WETA: www.colorincolorado.org.

Everything ESL. ESL resources for teaching English language learners K–12: www.everythingesl.net.

Language Castle. Resources for teaching dual language learners in preschool: www.languagecastle.com.

National Center on Cultural and Linguistic Responsiveness: http://eclkc.ohs.acf.hhs.gov/hslc/tta-system/cultural-linguistic.

National Clearinghouse for English Language Acquisition (NCELA): http://www.ncela.gwu.edu/.

## Online documents

Division for Early Childhood. 2010. Responsiveness to ALL children, families, and professionals: Integrating cultural and linguistic diversity into policy and practice. Position statement. Online: http://eclkc.ohs.acf.hhs.gov/hslc/tta-system/cultural-linguistic/Dual%20Language%20Learners/disabilities/inclusion/position-statement.pdf.

NAEYC. 1995. Responding to linguistic and cultural diversity: Recommendations for the education of young children. Washington, DC: Author. Online: www.naeyc.org/files/naeyc/file/positions/PSDIV98.PDF.

NAEYC. 2009. Where we stand on responding to linguistic and cultural diversity. Washington, DC: Author. Online: www.naeyc.org/files/naeyc/file/positions/diversity.pdf.

Teachers of English to Speakers of Other Languages (TESOL). 2010. Position paper on language and literacy development for young English language learners (ages 3–8). Online: www.tesol.org/s_tesol/bin.asp?CID=32&DID=371&DOC=FILE.PDF.

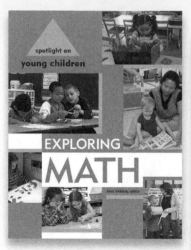

**Read the Spotlight on Young Children series—compilations from *Young Children* on key topics for early childhood educators.**

### Spotlight on Young Children: Exploring Math

*Amy Shillady, ed.*

It is important for teachers to incorporate mathematics into the daily curriculum to help ensure young children gain the foundational skills for later success in math. This book will help teachers learn about meaningful, authentic experiences that promote mathematical thinking from infancy through age 8.

**Item #: 367**

### Spotlight on Young Children and Nature

*Amy Shillady, ed.*

Nature exploration is fundamental to young children's curiosity, discovery, and sense of wonder—it supports their growth in all developmental domains. Teachers of children from infancy through age 8 will learn about using nature education to address early learning standards, to involve families and the community, and to encourage children's appreciation of the natural world.

**Item #: 294**

### Spotlight on Young Children and Families

*Derry Koralek, ed.*

Family involvement is critical to the success of young children in early learning environments and beyond. Educators must strive to acknowledge and value the many differences of each family. In this book authors address topics such as sharing the care of infants and toddlers, acknowledging culture and promoting inclusion, conferencing with families, and helping to support learning at home.

**Item #: 288**